Voyager Passport F

Fluency 2

ISBN 978-1-4168-0665-3

Copyright 2008 by Voyager Expanded Learning, L.P.

All rights reserved. No part of this publication may be reproduced or transmitted in any form or by any means, electronic or mechanical, including photocopy, recording, or any information storage and retrieval system, without permission in writing from the publisher.

Printed in the United States of America 08 09 10 11 12 13 DIG 9 8 7 6 5 4 3 2

Table of Contents

Amazing Stories
Independence Hall: The Birthplace of Our Country 1
My Day as a Junior Ranger 2
The Amazing Ben Franklin 3
What Will I Think of Next? 4
Writing the Constitution of the United States 5

Fitness
Kinds of Exercise 6
Move Toward Better Health with Aerobics Classes 7
My Very First Aerobics Class 8
The Soccer Game 9
The Most Popular Sport in the World. 10

Special Days
A Different Kind of New Year's Celebration 11
The Mardi Gras Parade 12
A Day to Wear Green 13
What a Day for a Birthday! 14
Passover: A Time for Traditions 15

Community Outreach
Helping Out at the Zoo 16
Big Brothers, Big Sisters—Making a Difference 17
A Bad Start to a Good Day 18
Meals on Wheels: A Special Delivery Service 19
Support the House Where Children Are First 20

Timed Passage 21
Timed Passage 22
Word List 23

Fluency Practice

 Read the story to each other.

 Read the story on your own.

 Read the story to your partner again. Try to read the story even better.

 Questions? Ask your partner two questions about the story. Tell each other about the story you just read.

Timed Reading

1. When you do a timed reading with your partner, make sure that you have practiced your story and know all the words.

2. When you are ready, tell your partner to start the timer.

3. Read carefully, and your partner will stop you at 1 minute. When you stop, mark your place.

4. Count the total number of words you read.

5. In the back of your Student Book, write the number of words you read and color in the squares on your Fluency Chart.

6. Now switch with your partner.

AMAZING STORIES

Independence Hall:
The Birthplace of Our Country

The birthplace of our country is a brick building with a tall steeple. It is in Philadelphia. For about 200 years, the Liberty Bell hung there. This building is interesting to look at. It is not famous for its style though. It is better known for what took place there.

A gifted gentleman planned the building. He wanted it to be his area's capitol. Later, he helped invent our country's government. (71) Many of the planning meetings took place in this hall. Our country's founders met there. They talked about which form of rule was best. It also is where they wrote many important papers.

Today, the hall is part of a history park. This park is popular with tourists. Each year, many people go there. They can see firsthand where our country was born. (134)

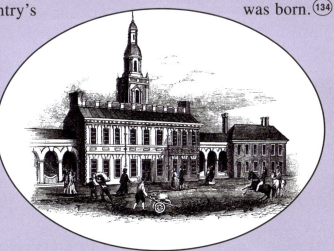

▶ **PASSAGE 2** AMAZING STORIES

My Day as a Junior Ranger

Yesterday during my class field trip, I was not just a student. I was a Junior Ranger for the day! My teacher learned about the Junior Ranger Program at a national park in Pennsylvania. She made sure we could take part in it for our field trip.

My class arrived at the park early in the day. Red, white, and blue banners waved at the park entrance. There, a ranger handed each student a booklet. (75) It was filled with things to do. There were questions to answer as we went through the park. We were challenged to collect six stamps during the day. I decided not to quit until I had all of them.

At the end of the day, a gentleman checked our books. He gave each of us a Junior Ranger badge. Being a Junior Ranger made the trip a lot of fun! (145)

AMAZING STORIES

The *Amazing* Ben Franklin

Ben Franklin was one of our country's early leaders. He was a gentleman of many talents. It seems he never quit using them!

Franklin started our country's first public library. He also started the first police force. He was a printer by trade. One book he printed was his own. This book was very popular. Readers around the world enjoyed it. In his book, Franklin gave honest advice. His statements were spiced with humor. (74)

Some would insist that Franklin had done enough. He did not slow down though. He turned his sights toward making new things. His famous kite-flying test led him to invent the lightning rod. He also had ideas for things from stoves to reading glasses.

Ben Franklin was a great man. He's a person you might want to learn more about. (135)

What Will I Think of Next?

I do not look forward to doing chores, and I'm always trying to find ways to make them easier. Last week, I invented a way to make polishing the floor easier. I stitched a dust cloth to the bottom of each of my socks, and then I sprayed each cloth with polish. When that was done, I skated back and forth across the floor. It was shiny and clean in no time!

Now I have a new idea. Can you guess what it is? I want to find a way to produce and sell my new cleaning product. I'm sure it will be a popular item. I could even sell it on those TV programs that feature new products.

Right now though, I have to quit dreaming. When I finish washing the dishes, I'll get back to making plans.

Writing the Constitution of the United States

It was summer. The weather was hot and humid. Inside a famous hall, gentlemen wearing wool suits came together to plan a new country.

Tall windows captured a few gentle breezes. Banners in the room moved slowly to and fro. These breezes were welcome, but the poor men had to close the windows. They feared that people listening outside would spread tales about what they were discussing.

For four months, the men worked in the steamy hall. They listened to one another's ideas. They spoke their own. Finally, they agreed on a plan of rule for their new country. It was called the Constitution of the United States. It was long and complete. It took two days to write it in final form.

That plan has stood the test of time. It is the plan we use today and one that many other countries have copied.

PASSAGE 1

Kinds of Exercise

Regular exercise is good for you. There are many kinds of exercise. You can choose the type that fits your needs.

Some people like to lift weights. This exercise builds muscles. Over time, people must adjust their weights. They are stronger, so the weights must be heavier. This helps the person become even stronger!

Yoga is good for muscles too. A lot of people practice yoga. ⁶⁶ They do a lot of stretching moves. Yoga helps build strength, and it also helps people relax.

Aerobic exercise is good for the heart. It helps people build endurance. Swimming is a good example of this kind of exercise.

Clearly, there are many kinds of exercise. You must like the exercise you choose though. That's why it is important to choose the one that is right for you. ¹³⁴

Move Toward Better Health with Aerobics Classes

Aerobic exercise has captured the imagination of our nation. In fact, classes are in demand in most towns and cities. People who take these classes build strength. They also build endurance.

These classes are popular for many reasons. There are classes for all skill levels. Each class is led by a teacher. Music plays while the teacher shows the way to move. There are different types of classes from which to choose.(72) Many are based on dancing. Others use step platforms. Some let people ride in place on bicycles.

Do you want to take a class? Here are some things to remember. Start with a beginner's class. This lets you adjust slowly to the program. Be sure to stretch regularly before class. This will keep you from getting hurt.

Aerobics classes are a great idea. You can have fun and get healthy at the same time!(146)

PASSAGE 3 — FITNESS

My Very First Aerobics Class

I know that regular exercise is part of a healthy lifestyle. That's why I wanted to take an aerobics class. The classes are in high demand, but I found one at the gym near my house.

To persuade Mom to let me go, I promised to do chores to pay for the class. She said it was fine as long as she walked there with me.

I arrived early the first day. While I waited, I imagined what the class would be like. (83) Soon, the teacher came in. She put on a slow song and showed us how to stretch, reminding us to breathe deeply as we moved.

Then, the music sped up, and the whole class was in motion. The songs continued one after another. The teacher commented that this was a good endurance exercise.

Finally, the class was over. I felt great! I decided to ask Mom to join me next time. She would like it too. (159)

The Soccer Game

It was a gray morning, but Sara was excited in spite of the weather. As goalkeeper for her soccer team, Sara's job was to prevent the other team from scoring. She jumped up and down to loosen her muscles. Sara knew she needed to be ready to leap and slide to keep the ball out of the net.

As the game started, Sara watched her team kick the ball down the field. The other team captured the ball and moved it toward her. Sara tensed. She watched as the ball flew toward her. She adjusted her position and stretched out her arms. She blocked the ball! People cheered, and Sara felt great. She relaxed and settled down to play the rest of the game.

When the match ended, Sara's team had scored only once. However, because of Sara's defense, the other team had not scored at all. Sara's team had won!

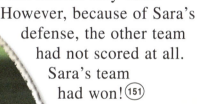

The Most Popular Sport in the World

There is a game played all over the world. In most countries, it's known as football. Do you know the other name for this game? It's soccer. More people play and watch soccer than almost all other sports combined. That is why it is called the most popular sport in the world.

Soccer is played by two teams, with 7 to 11 players on each team. The point of the game is to move the ball over the other team's goal line. Players must do this using any part of their bodies except their arms and hands. The team that scores the most goals in 90 minutes is the winner.

Every four years, soccer teams from around the world compete in the World Cup. This is a big soccer tournament. Each team wants the title of best soccer team in the world.

If you don't know about soccer, then attend a game. Maybe you'll understand why it's so popular!

SPECIAL DAYS

PASSAGE 1

A Different Kind of New Year's Celebration

Every winter, excitement fills the air for 15 days. It is Chinese New Year. Chinese people around the world enjoy this time.

During Chinese New Year, people are happy and cheerful. One reason is that everyone has a birthday party at this time! It doesn't matter when they were born. Families give thanks for the past year. They pray for good things in the year to come. People also honor their ancestors. ⁷² They show how they admire them during this time.

The last night of Chinese New Year is special. There is a big street party. The street is decorated with bright lanterns. People play drums and dance. A long paper dragon winds among the people. The sound of firecrackers fills the night.

The street party always is fun. It is a great way to end the long holiday and a wonderful way to start the new year. ¹⁴⁸

11

The Mardi Gras Parade

Marta's teacher told the class about the holiday called Mardi Gras. She explained that *Mardi Gras* means "Fat Tuesday" in French. She said that it is called Carnival in many parts of the world. People dress up in costumes and masks and have a party. There are many parades.

Today, the class was going to such a parade. People lined the avenue. Colorful flags decorated the buildings. Marta admired the bands that led the parade. Drums resounded in a steady beat. Horns played catchy tunes. Then, the floats began to roll by. Cheerful people threw plastic beads and coins from the floats. Marta squeezed her way to the front of the crowd. She was able to catch many "treasures."

By the end of the parade, she had caught several necklaces. Her pockets were filled with brightly colored coins. It had been exciting. Marta already was looking forward to next year's parade.

SPECIAL DAYS

PASSAGE 3

A Day to Wear Green

On March 17, be sure to wear the color green. If you don't, you might get pinched! Can you guess the name of this playful holiday? It is called St. Patrick's Day.

St. Patrick's Day is named for an Irish priest. It is celebrated widely in Ireland. Many American cities also observe the day. It is a lot like a carnival. People gather to have fun. Some city streets are lined with parades. (73) The parade in New York City is very big. Police direct traffic away from the parade avenues. Viewers admire the bands and the floats.

On this day, people decorate with the color green. Sometimes they even color their food and drinks. Would you like a glass of green milk? What would you think about a green cookie for dessert?

On St. Patrick's Day, everyone is said to be Irish. So grab some green milk and cookies and have a great time! (154)

13

What a Day for a Birthday!

It was Tuesday, April 1, and it was Paco's birthday. His mother had baked a cake and made snacks.

"This will be a fantastic party!" thought Paco, as his friends began to arrive.

His mother put the cake on the table. Ten candles twinkled on top. Everyone began singing "Happy Birthday to You." When they finished, Paco took a deep breath and tried to blow out the candles. They stayed lit! Paco cheerfully tried again, but the candles kept burning.

"What is going on?" laughed Paco, as he blew again and again.

Finally, someone yelled, "April Fool's!" and everyone laughed.

Now Paco understood. These were trick candles. He had forgotten it was April Fool's Day.

"That was a really good trick," Paco laughed. Then, he turned back toward the cake.

Paco hoped he still had time to play a trick on someone. In fact, that's the wish he would make if only he could blow out those candles.

SPECIAL DAYS

Passage 5

Passover: A Time for Traditions

Jewish people around the world celebrate Passover each spring. They recall a time long ago when Jews were freed from slavery.

There are things to do before the holiday begins. Families must make their homes ready. First, they put away their regular dishes. Special ones are used during this time. Then, they look for all the bread in the house. They must give it away. They replace it with a flat bread. It is a symbol of the season. (79)

The holiday always begins the same way. People gather at the table. A family member reads a certain story. Then, everyone eats dinner. It is made up of special foods. Each food has a meaning. One of these is greens dipped in salt water. The water stands for the slaves' tears from long ago.

Passover is an important holiday for Jewish people. It is a time of peace. It also is a time to remember. (154)

15

Helping Out at the Zoo

A few days each month, my mother volunteers at the zoo. Last week she said I could help too. That made me happy! The zoo is one of my favorite places. I love animals, and it was exciting to think I could help take care of them.

When we got to the zoo, we learned that our job was to help feed the elephants. We set off to find the zookeeper. The first thing he did when we joined him was to herd the elephants into a feeding barn. Such large animals sometimes can be dangerous, so he did this job by himself.

Our job was to bring the hay into the barn. To do this, we needed a tractor. Mom drove the tractor, and I sat beside her. We loaded bales of hay and then took them to the area where the elephants like to eat.

Helping at the zoo is difficult work, but I like knowing that I am helping the animals. Someday I hope to feed the elephants all by myself!

Big Brothers, Big Sisters—
Making a Difference

How Big Brothers, Big Sisters Started

Big Brothers, Big Sisters started almost 100 years ago. Some adults saw children with difficult lives. Many of the children were poor. Others lived in dangerous places. Some were getting into trouble with the law. These adults had an idea. They would form friendships with these children. The adults called themselves "big brothers" or "big sisters." The children were called "little brothers" or "little sisters."

How Big Brothers, Big Sisters Helps

The program pairs caring adults with needy children.⁸⁵ The adults act as role models. They help the children set and reach goals. The children can talk about themselves. This helps them learn to express their ideas. Along the way, the pairs have a lot of fun!

What Big and Little Brothers and Sisters Do Together

The pairs do many things. Some visit museums. Others go to libraries. Many play sports. Activities can be as simple as going for a walk. The idea is to spend time with each other.

It is easy to see why Big Brothers, Big Sisters is so popular. It provides fun and builds character for adults and children alike.¹⁹⁰

A Bad Start to a Good Day

It was a rainy October day. The school bus crept down the slick, dangerous road.

"I'm afraid we'll be late," the driver shouted over his shoulder. "This weather is slowing us down!"

The children's choir was on its way to a nursing home. They sang at a different one every month. The children liked to express themselves this way. It was one of their favorite things to do.

Finally, the difficult drive was over, and the bus delivered them to the nursing home. It was warm and bright inside.

The residents were in good health, and they were happy to see the children.

"Where is the piano?" the choir leader asked. That's when they got the news that there was no piano.

The choir had not practiced singing without music. For a moment, they thought they might have to cancel the show. Then, an older man of good character offered to play his guitar while the choir sang.

During the day, many new friendships were made. For a day that started so badly, it turned out to be one of the best days ever!

COMMUNITY OUTREACH

PASSAGE 4

Meals on Wheels: A Special Delivery Service

Early Days for Meals on Wheels

Meals on Wheels started in England during the Second World War. Many homes were damaged by the war. People in those homes no longer had a way to cook. Some volunteers began taking hot meals to the needy. Over time, the service grew.

Soon, the program began in the United States. Here, it had a different purpose, which was to serve elderly and disabled people. It also served people who were ill.

Meals on Wheels Today

Today, Meals on Wheels is in almost every town. ⑨¹ Because of this, people in need can enjoy their favorite foods at home. Volunteers run the program. Everyone works without getting paid. They plan the meals, buy the food, and run the service with money that people give them.

Helping Meals on Wheels

Anyone who wants to reach out to others can help. Those who like to cook are needed to prepare the meals. Jobs such as packing the food and cleaning are easy and rewarding. Of course, good drivers are wanted to take the food to the people who need it. Whatever your talent, there's a place for you at Meals on Wheels! ⑱⁹⁵

Support the House Where Children Are First

A Ronald McDonald House is a special place. It is a home away from home for families with sick children. Ill children sometimes have to travel a long way for care. They also may need to spend time in a hospital.

Ronald McDonald Houses are located near hospitals. They give families of sick children a place to rest. For a small fee, families can have a comfortable room. Best of all, they are near the hospital where their sick child is being treated.

The houses also offer a place to relax. Most houses have a nice, large living area. There are games to play there. There are books to read. Families staying at the house can gather in this room. Their ill children can spend time with them away from the hospital. Children can play together. Parents can give one another support.

In many cities, Ronald McDonald Houses also offer classes. They teach mothers-to-be how to stay healthy. They also teach parents how to raise healthy, happy children.

How can you help Ronald McDonald House? Here are a few ideas for things to give:

- toys or games
- canned food
- healthy snacks
- paper goods
- money

With your help, we can make sure there is a place where children are first!

Calling All Teachers

Are you looking for a field trip that is fun and educational? Consider a trip to the Brooklyn Children's Museum. This was the first museum created just for young people. It was started more than 100 years ago.

The museum is filled with hands-on exhibits. Students can touch and explore each one. Some are from the museum's collection. Some are on loan from other museums. First, take your class to see the cultural collection. They will see ancient combs and dolls. Next, take them to see the natural history collection. It includes a whale bone and the complete skeleton of an Asian elephant! Last, end the tour with some free time. Your students can entertain themselves by exploring parts of the museum on their own.

If you plan to attend an exhibit during the week, call ahead. We will arrange a class tour of the museum. Workshops also can be arranged.

What a Night!

Lisa walked up the steps that led from the subway station to the streets of New York. As she held her mother's hand tightly, she smiled excitedly. "I'm going to attend my first play on Broadway," she thought.

Lisa's heart began pounding as soon as she sat down in her seat in the theater. A few minutes later, the curtain opened, and a man walked quickly to the microphone. He greeted the audience. Then, the lights were lowered, and the play started.

The play was a musical called *Oklahoma!* It was set during the last century in a small town. The story told about the lives of the men and women who lived there. The play was very entertaining.

When the play ended, the audience stood and clapped loudly. Lisa felt sad to know that the play was over. Yet, she also felt excited. She had made an important decision during the play. "Mom," she said happily as they left the theater, "I've decided to become an actress and a singer when I grow up."

Word List

popular	difference
spread	finished
exercise	interest
muscles	gone
imagine	known
length	nothing